THE BIG BOOK OF SANTA

MARY ENGELBREIT

THE BIG BOOK OF SANTA

MARY ENGELBREIT

Andrews McMeel
Publishing®

a division of Andrews McMeel Universal

I love Christmas, and everything that goes along with it! The decorations, the music, the school Christmas pageants, the homemade ornaments, the food—and of course I'm referring to the cookies—all of it! So much of Christmas is tied up in memories from childhood, and they all come flooding back at Christmas time, probably none stronger than our thoughts of Santa Claus. What power he has to evoke all these wonderful memories! That's why I never get tired of drawing him— in his sleigh, in the woods, in a castle, with children, with animals, with elves and snowmen . . . Every year, he reminds me again to BELIEVE. What more magical power could there be, and how lucky am I to get to try and draw that magic every year??!

Wishing you and yours the power to believe again this year!

Mary

The Good List

HEIGH HO, the HOLLY

ISN'T CHRISTMAS JOLLY?

Holly Wreath Santa

Big Santa Face

Christmas, children, is not a date—
It's a state of mind.

·Mary Ellen Chase·

Christmas State of Mind

North Pole in Mouseland

'Twas the Night Before Christmas

HAD I BUT ONE PENNY IN THE WORLD, THOU SHOULDST HAVE IT FOR GINGERBREAD.

WM · SHAKESPEARE

Penny Gingerbread

Christmas Circus

Less Egg! More Nog!

Cherry Christmas

Man in the Winter Moon

Santa Dropping In

The Animals' Christmas

Believe

King of the Year

Cookies for Me? No Kidding?!

December Hugs

Snowmen Soldiers

Santa's Sleigh

CHRISTMAS IS COMING

RUN AWAY! RUN AWAY!

Run Away Christmas

Santa Says Hello

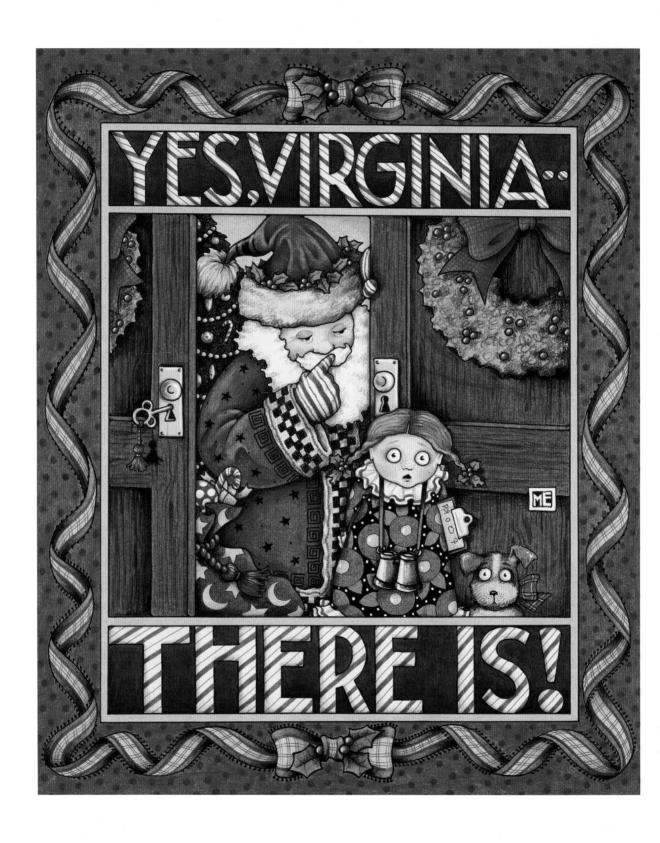

Yes, Virginia...There Is

Cheer

HO HO HO .

Fat Santa

Jolly Old Saint Nick

Cherry Santa

Santa's Sleigh Ride

BLESSED IS THE SEASON
WHICH ENGAGES THE WHOLE WORLD
IN A CONSPIRACY OF LOVE

♥ Hamilton Wright Mabie ♥

Ring Around the Santa

The Joymakers

Santa

Hodely Ho

Santa Marches On

'TIS CHRISTMAS TELLS THE MERRIEST TALE!

Santa, What a Bag

Christmas Is in Full Swing

Santa Snowflake

He's Making a List

Ho Ho Ho Santa

Christmas Pageant Fun

Yet Another Christmas Pageant

Candy Santa

OPEN YOUR HEART~
OPEN IT WIDE;
SOMEONE IS STANDING OUTSIDE

It Can't Hurt to Ask

Santa With Toys

Santa and Snow Boys

Let the Merrymaking Begin

Christmas Blow Ups

Countdown to Christmas

Claus and Effect

Santa and Holly

Hi, Honey, I'm Home

May Your
Christmas
be a Happy One
And may the
New Year bring
you
Contentment
and Prosperity
in overflowing
measure.

Christmas Sentiment

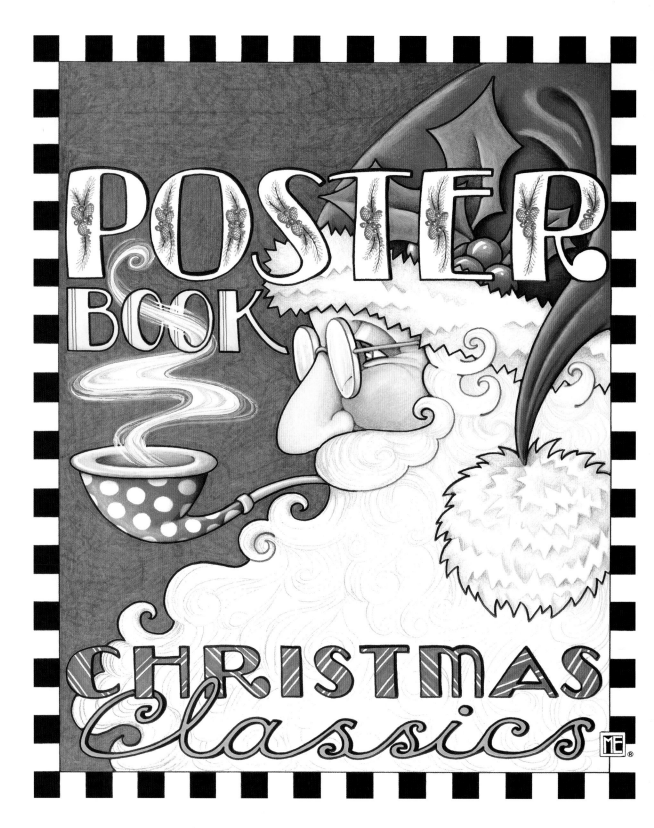

Believe II

The Annual Christmas Production

Christmas Show Today 5¢ or 1 Candy Cane

Todays Show "SANTA TAKES A HOLIDAY"

DON'T GET YOUR TINSEL IN A TANGLE!

Santa Letter

S.S. Claus

Is Christmas Fun or What?

Santa and Elves Photo

On Christmas Play

Give Your Heart

FROM ALL OF US

Some cause HAPPINESS wherever they go.
···OSCAR WILDE···

Check Cherry Santa

Wishes

Merry Christmas

Ho Ho Ho

Father Christmas

Santa Over the Rooftops

Sunburned Santa

Chimney Squeeze

Christmas Is Coming

Bearded Breit Santa

The Christmas Wizard

Claustrophobia

Toyland Express

Santa Baby

Russian Santa

·THE CHRISTMAS GARDEN·

Santa's Garden

Christmas Dudes

Wonder of Christmas

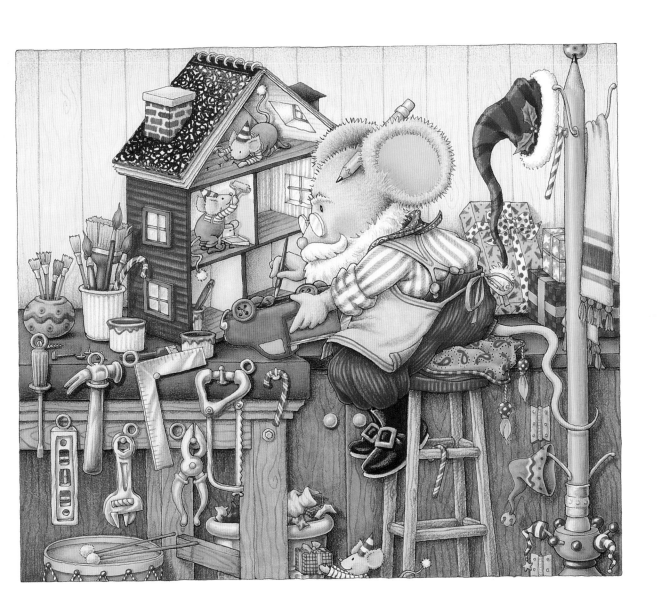

Santa Mouse Dollhouse

THE MAN OF THE HOUR

The Man of the Hour

Santa's Gathering

Starry Santa

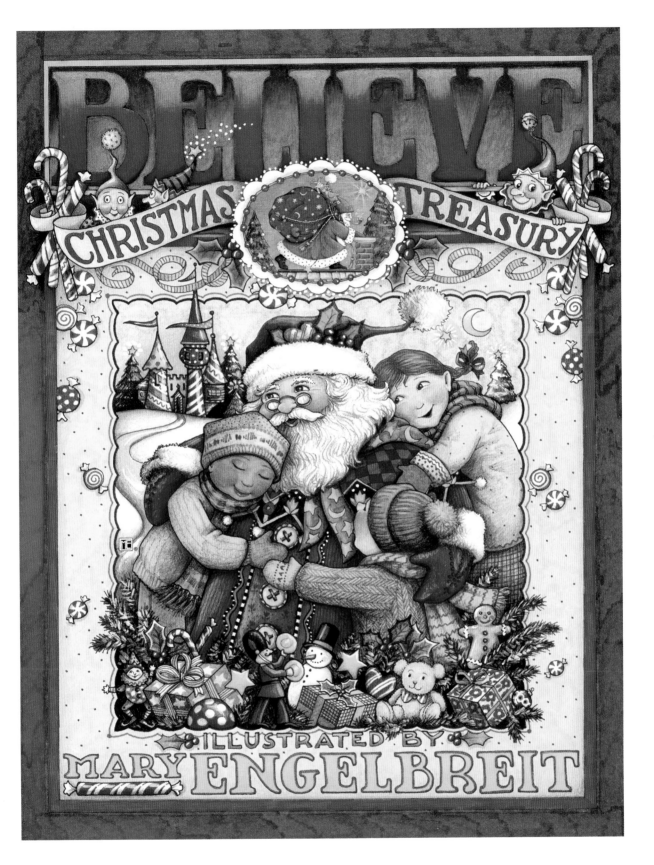

Christmas Treasury

O Christmas Tree Santa

The BIG BOOK of SANTA

Andrews McMeel Publishing
a division of Andrews McMeel Universal
1130 Walnut Street, Kansas City, Missouri 64106

www.andrewsmcmeel.com

16 17 18 19 20 SDB 10 9 8 7 6 5 4 3 2 1

ISBN: 978-1-4494-8058-5

Library of Congress Control Number: 2016934553

ATTENTION: SCHOOLS AND BUSINESSES

Andrews McMeel books are available at quantity discounts with bulk
purchase for educational, business, or sales promotional use. For information,
please e-mail the Andrews McMeel Publishing Special Sales Department:
specialsales@amuniversal.com.